W9-BUE-243

DATE DUE		
APR 28 '95		
MAY 12 '06		
DEC 16 '9?		
DEC 25 '97		
MAR 30 '98		
MAY 9 9 '3		
JUN 3 02		

$14.00

394.2
BUR   Burns, Diane L.
              Arbor Day

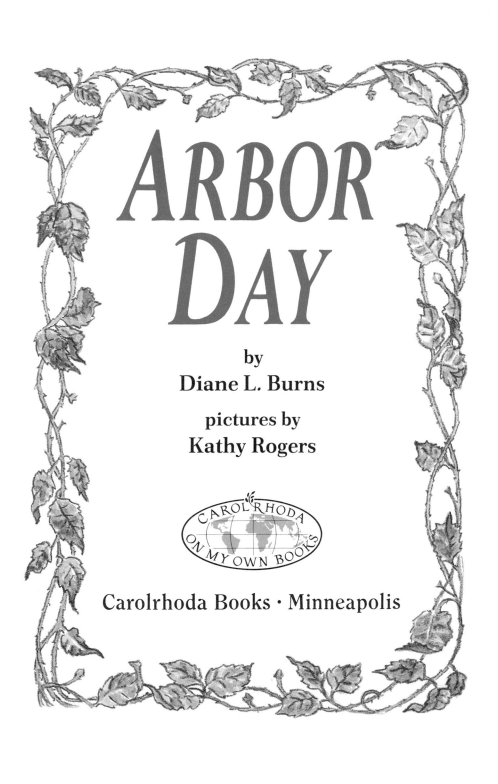

ARBOR DAY

by
Diane L. Burns

pictures by
Kathy Rogers

Carolrhoda Books · Minneapolis

*To my sister, Laurie, and those who planted
with us: Chuck, Bob, and Margaret Anne*

Library of Congress Cataloging-in-Publication Data

Burns, Diane L.
 Arbor Day / by Diane Burns ; pictures by Kathy Rogers ;
illustrations by Kathy Rogers.
  p. cm. — (Carolrhoda on my own book)
 Summary: Describes the history of Arbor Day and how it is
celebrated.
 ISBN 0-87614-346-X (lib. bdg.)
 1. Arbor Day — United States — Juvenile literature. [1. Arbor
Day.] I. Rogers, Kathy, ill. II. Title. III. Series.
SD363.B87   1989
394.2'6 — dc19   88-31706
                                                      CIP
                                                       AC

Manufactured in the United States of America

    3 4 5 6 7 8 9 10 99 98 97 96 95 94 93 92

Trees are important in our world.
Earth's oldest, biggest, and
tallest living things are trees.

3

There are about twenty thousand
different kinds of trees.
Trees help the earth.

The leaves of trees
add oxygen to the air.
Oxygen is what we need to breathe.
Leaves also clean the air.
Fallen leaves add food to the soil,
helping other plants to grow.

Tree roots help the forest floor
hold water for other plants to use.
Roots of trees stop dirt
from washing away in floods
and snowslides, and from
blowing away in strong winds.

Birds and animals use trees for homes and food and resting places. People use parts of trees to make homes and food too.

Children like climbing in trees
and camping under them.
We all enjoy looking at trees.
We rest in their cool shade.

When settlers came to America
during the 1600s, they were surprised
to find so many trees.
There were trees as far
as a person could see.
There were trees so huge
that a large man could not
put his arms around one.

Those trees helped the pioneer
families survive.
Wood fires and log homes kept them
warm and safe.
From the wood of the trees,

pioneers made furniture,
barrels, and tools.
Wood, bark, leaves, sap, and fruit
gave them paper, ink, medicines, food,
and even padding for their beds.

Most people thought the forests
would last forever.
By 1800, though, America had its first
wood shortage.
How did it happen?
People had not known that trees
were being cut down faster
than new ones could grow.
As more and more people came
to America, they used more and more
wood for things they needed.
Farmers cut down whole forests
to make room to plant crops.
Lumberjacks cut the best trees
and left the others.
When the lumberjacks moved on,
some kinds of trees
did not grow back.

During the early 1800s,
only a few people thought about
replacing the cut-down trees.
John Chapman did.
He traveled westward,
from Pennsylvania to Illinois,

planting apple orchards.
He gave away apple seeds
and seedlings—small, young trees—
to settlers.
The settlers nicknamed him
Johnny Appleseed.

Johnny met Chief Cornplanter,
a Seneca Indian who also worked with trees.
Chief Cornplanter taught Johnny
how to make an apple tree
grow two kinds of apple fruit.
This method is called grafting,
and many people use it today
to care for their trees.
Johnny and the Chief also traded seeds.
The trees that grew from their seeds
helped people for many years.

Some American men made trips
to foreign countries.
There they saw ruined forests
and learned how forestland
could be protected.
They came back to the United States
and told people what they had learned.
They warned that if Americans
didn't use trees more carefully,
someday the forests would all be gone.
People were not ready to listen.
Years went by, and America's forests
kept disappearing.
Finally, the man who is remembered as
the father of Arbor Day
got people to listen.

On a summer day in 1867,
J. Sterling Morton stood
outside his home in Nebraska.
No tree leaves whispered
in the wind.
No shade cooled the hot ground.

Morton sighed.

He had grown up in Michigan,
where there were a lot of trees.
There had never been many trees
in Nebraska.

Morton knew that trees
help the land in many ways.
Maybe something could be done about
Nebraska's treeless plains.
Maybe *he* could do something.
Morton was the editor of
Nebraska's first newspaper.
He used his paper to tell people
about the need for trees.
The country was just starting to
practice conservation.
Conservation means taking care of
trees, animals, land, water, and air.

J. Sterling Morton hoped
that the people of Nebraska
would care about trees.
He named April 10, 1872,
Tree-Planting Day, or Arbor Day.
Arbor is a Latin word that means tree.
Morton soon found that
people did care.
Over a million trees were planted
in Nebraska on this special day!
After that year, people planted
more trees every spring.
In 1885, Nebraskans moved
their tree-planting day to
Morton's birthday, April 22,
and made it a state holiday.

For a long time, Nebraska was known
as The Tree-Planters' State.
Today, the Nebraska National Forest
covers over 200,000 acres.
It is one of the world's biggest forests
planted by people.
Nebraska has so many trees,
it sends seedlings around the world
to places that need them!

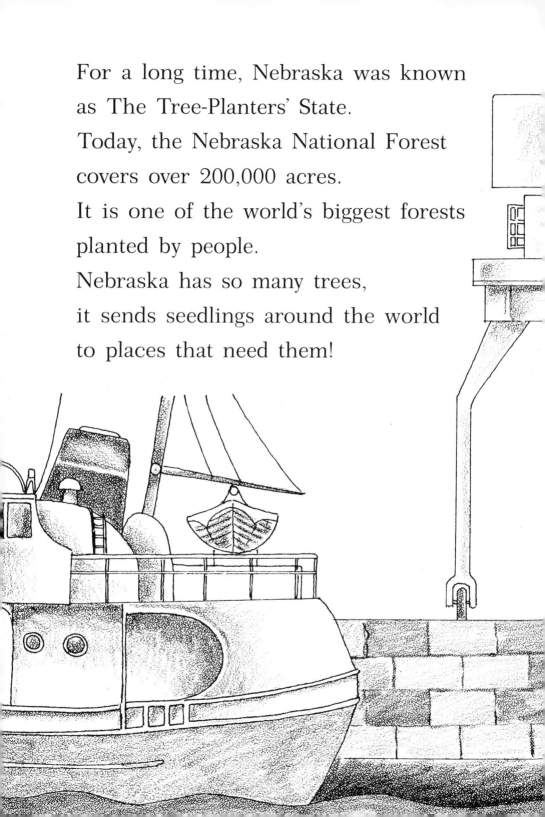

Morton worked to make Arbor Day
a national holiday.
He wrote and spoke to many people
about the importance of tree planting.
Kansas, Tennessee, and Minnesota
were the first states to try
Nebraska's good idea.
Fifteen years after the first
Arbor Day, over 300 million trees and
vines had been planted in America.

Countries like England, Spain, and
Canada thought Arbor Day was
a good idea too.
In 1887, England celebrated its first
Arbor Day by planting shade trees

in patterns that spelled words.

In 1896, King Alfonso of Spain planted
a young pine tree during his country's
first Arbor Day celebration,
which was called *Fiesta del Arbol.*

Children have always helped
with Arbor Day celebrations.
In 1882, Cincinnati schoolchildren
were part of a huge
Arbor Day festival.
After speeches and parades,
the children planted many trees
in a city park.
Those trees are still growing.
On Arbor Day, 1888, New York children
planted the state flower—the rose—and the
state tree—the white elm—in Central Park.

When J. Sterling Morton died in 1902,
people around the world were
saddened by the news.
Some Americans decided to remember
the father of Arbor Day

by making a statue of him.
Children in other countries
heard that people of all ages
were giving money to help build it.
They sent their money to help too.
Today, the statue can be
seen at Morton's home—
Arbor Lodge—in Nebraska.

During the early 1900s,
President Theodore Roosevelt
continued J. Sterling Morton's work.
He cared about trees too.
Roosevelt said that a forest
doesn't just *have* wood.
It makes new wood.
President Roosevelt set aside
a million acres for
national forestlands.

About this same time,
Gifford Pinchot became America's
first trained expert on forests.
Pinchot studied in Europe
because America did not yet have
any forestry schools.
He learned that forests need more
than sunlight and water.
They need to be protected from large fires
and from some animals and people.
They need space to grow
tall and straight.
They need little trees to replace
the big ones that are cut down.
When the U.S. Forest Service
was started in 1905
to protect forests for the future,
Pinchot was its first leader.

Gifford Pinchot and Teddy Roosevelt
worked together.
They taught people that trees can be
grown and harvested as crops.
They were a good team.
Together, they began many
conservation programs.

Planting trees by hand
takes a lot of time.
During the 1940s, the Forest Service
began using helicopters and airplanes
to drop seeds to the ground.
Birds and mice ate a lot of the seeds.

Today, tree seeds dropped from planes
are coated with something
that tastes bad to animals
but does not harm them or the seeds.

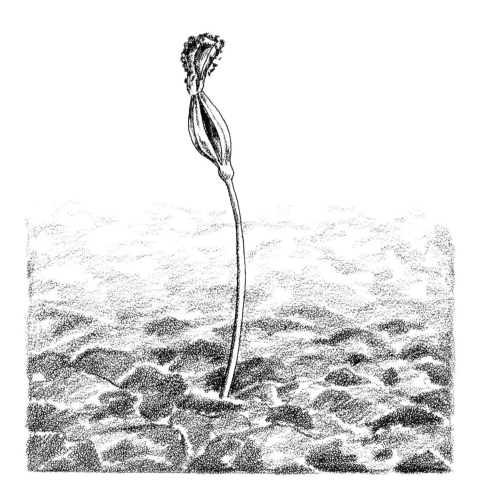

Still, most trees are planted by hand
or by a plow-like machine
often pulled by a tractor.

Some states hire people each year
who move from place to place
planting trees.
These crews work fast.
One very skilled person can
hand-plant one thousand trees a day!

On Arbor Day, Americans
celebrate trees in many ways.
Schoolchildren still plant seedlings
to remind people of
Arbor Day's importance.
They read stories and poetry
about trees.
Each Arbor Day, the president,
or someone chosen by the president,
plants a tree on the
White House grounds.

Arbor Day is celebrated
in many countries.
In the United States where it began,
Arbor Day is not
a national celebration.
Four states have made Arbor Day
a public holiday: Nebraska, Utah,
Wyoming, and Florida.
Alaska does not have Arbor Day at all.
Others celebrate Arbor Day
on different days of the year.
Depending on their planting season,
some have it in spring,
and some have it in autumn.
In most states, Arbor Day is
the last Friday in April.
Many people want this day to be
the national Arbor Day.

Conservationists—who work to protect
trees, animals, land, water, and air—
say that this national holiday would
make more people aware
of the importance of trees.
They think that every year
people should be reminded that
we need to take care of our forests.

Arbor Day is a day
that makes people think.
We remember the many ways
trees have helped people in the past
and are helping them today.
Arbor Day also helps us
think of the future.
When we plant a tree, we leave
something for other people to enjoy
for many years to come.

PLANT YOUR OWN TREE
FOR ARBOR DAY!

Here's how:

1. Choose a place where the tree will get sunlight and not be stepped upon. Get permission from the landowner.
2. Plant the tree in the spring, just before it starts to grow for the summer, or in the fall, after it has stopped growing.

3. Carry the tree gently. Keep the roots wet and covered with material so the wind and sun can't harm them.
4. Dig a hole a little bigger than the bundle of roots so they will have room to grow. Set the dirt aside.
5. Uncover the roots. Kneel down, and with one hand, hold the tree in the center of the hole. The roots should not be too deep or too close to the hole's top.
6. With your other hand, carefully push some of the saved soil into the hole and pack it around the roots. Take care not to break the root stems.
7. Water the tree well. Then fill the hole with more soil. Press it firmly to remove air pockets around the roots. Water again.

There—you've planted a tree for the future! If you plant more than one, leave at least six feet of space around each tree. And remember, trees grow slowly, so be patient.

To get a young tree for planting, contact your state Department of Natural Resources. You can also write to:

The National Arbor Day Association
100 Arbor Avenue
Nebraska City, NE 68410

The author gratefully acknowledges encouragement from the following sources in the preparation of this manuscript: Caroline Arnold and Jo Borack, who provided research information, and Judy Lehne and Tina Tibbitts for proofreading. Thanks also to the Rhinelander Public Library staff, especially Vivian Trewick and Kris Adams Wendt; to my husband, Phil, Forester Mike Beaufeaux, and Forest Entomologist William Kearby for their insights; and to Cathy Amberger and Joann Williams of the American Forestry Association, Forester Dick Cutler, and the National Arbor Day Foundation for their cheerful help.